Gonzalez Boys   Oct. 2020

Gonzalez Boys   Oct. 2020

TOP OF THE FOOD CHAIN

POLAR BEAR

KILLER KING OF THE ARCTIC

LOUISE SPILSBURY

WINDMILL
BOOKS™
New York

Published in 2014 by Windmill Books, An Imprint of Rosen Publishing
29 East 21st Street, New York, NY 10010

Produced for Windmill by Calcium Creative Ltd
Editor for Calcium Creative Ltd: Sarah Eason
US Editor: Sara Howell
Designers: Paul Myerscough and Keith Williams

Picture credits: Dreamstime: Akinshin 17t, Amuzica 27, Freezingpictures 26, Gentoomultimedia 17b, Lukyslukys 9t, Mirage3 25, Outdoorsman 15t, 22, 23t, 24, 28, Tbarrat 14, Visceralimage 29; Shutterstock: BMJ 5t, 13b, Jo Crebbin 11t, FloridaStock 7b, Gillmar 6, Cindy Haggerty 18, Hayati Kayhan cover, S. Kuelcue 13t, Marques 19, Vladimir Melnik 4, Miles Away Photography 14, Near and Far Photography 20, Kotomiti Okuma 8, Optimarc 11b, Outdoorsman 21, Stefan Redel 7t, Robert Sarosiek 9b, Sergey Uryadnikov 5b, 16, 23b, VikOl 1, 12, Wild Arctic Pictures 10.

Library of Congress Cataloging-in-Publication Data

Spilsbury, Louise.
  Polar bear : killer king of the Arctic / by Louise Spilsbury.
      pages cm. — (Top of the food chain)
  Includes index.
  ISBN 978-1-61533-739-2 (library binding) — ISBN 978-1-61533-795-8 (pbk.) — ISBN 978-1-61533-796-5
  1. Polar bear—Juvenile literature. 2. Predatory animals—Arctic regions—Juvenile literature. I. Title.
  QL737.C27S65 2014
  599.786—dc23
                          2013002094

Manufactured in the United States of America

CPSIA Compliance Information: Batch #BS13WM: For Further Information contact Windmill Books, New York, New York at 1-866-478-0556

CONTENTS

KING OF THE ICE

The polar bear is king of the ice in the **Arctic**. This is the area around the North Pole. It is a bitterly cold wilderness, covered with ice and snow and blasted by powerful winds. Polar bears are powerful **predators** that live among floating ice sheets in the Arctic Ocean and hunt in the freezing water along the coast.

A **food chain** shows the living things that eat each other within one **habitat**. At the bottom of most Arctic food chains are tiny plants and **algae** that make their own food using **energy** from the Sun. They are eaten by tiny animals, called **zooplankton**, which are then eaten by bigger creatures such as Arctic cod.

Polar bears live on the Arctic ice and swim the Arctic Ocean.

Links in the Food Chain

Polar bears are at the top of Arctic food chains. One polar bear food chain begins with algae, which are eaten by shrimp. Arctic cod eat shrimp and bearded seals eat the cod. Polar bears eat the seals. No animals eat the mighty polar bear!

Bearded seals are hunted and eaten by polar bears.

Polar bears usually live and hunt alone.

ARCTIC GIANT

It's no surprise that polar bears are kings of the Arctic. These mighty animals are the biggest of all bears, and are the largest of all predators on land. When a male polar bear stands up on its two back legs it can be 10 feet (3 m) tall. That's the same height as a one-story building! These giant predators can weigh as much as a small car.

Polar bears use their weight and strength to knock down big **prey** such as seals. They are so heavy that they could easily crack the ice beneath them when **stalking** prey across ice sheets. To prevent this, the bear's huge paws act like snowshoes to spread its weight across the ice beneath it.

Look how big an adult male polar bear is compared to a person! Female polar bears are about half the size of males.

A polar bear's paws can measure up to 12 inches (31 cm) across. That's as big as a large dinner plate! A polar bear can flip large seals out of the sea with just a single swipe from one of its massive paws.

Polar bear paws have claws that dig into the snow like ice picks!

To stop ice from cracking, polar bears spread their legs and lower their bodies when stalking prey on thin ice.

LIFE ON THE ICE

Polar bears are built for life on the ice, where winter temperatures can drop to a bone-chilling -50°F (-45°C). They are covered in a thick layer of fat, called **blubber**, which holds in the bear's body heat.

Polar bears also have two layers of fur, which provide amazing **insulation** from the cold. The outer layer prevents the inner fur from getting wet when the polar bear is in the ocean. After a swim, polar bears just give their fur a quick shake and it is nearly dry! Polar bears even have fur on their feet to protect them from the icy Arctic surfaces.

A polar bear's layer of fatty blubber is up to 4 inches (10 cm) thick.

Links in the Food Chain

Ringed seals dive up to 300 feet (90 m) deep and stay underwater for up to 45 minutes while catching shellfish and fish such as Arctic cod. The seals are named for the light-colored circular patterns on their dark gray backs.

Ringed seals are the smallest and most common seals in the Arctic.

Polar bears have a small tail and little ears to help stop them from losing heat.

CAMOUFLAGED

The polar bear's thick, white fur helps to keep this predator at the top of its food chain. Polar bears are so big and heavy that they cannot run quickly for long, so they save energy by sneaking up on prey. A white coat **camouflages** the bears by helping them to blend in with the Arctic snow and ice.

Although it appears to be white, in fact, polar bear fur is not white at all! Each hair is see-through and hollow. The hairs scatter and reflect light, which makes them look white. This process allows light to pass through the fur to the polar bear's black skin beneath, so the skin can absorb warmth from the Sun's rays.

In a land full of snow and ice, appearing white makes polar bears harder to spot!

A polar bear's eyes are brown and positioned close together.

A polar bear's eyes are small so they do not break up the white camouflage of the bear's body when its head is lowered against snow and ice. Like most predators, the bear's eyes are at the front of its head to help it judge how far away prey is.

Each long polar bear hair is like a thin, clear, plastic straw that reflects sunlight.

STALKING PREY

When a polar bear spots a seal resting on ice, it starts to crawl toward it. If the seal looks around, the polar bear holds itself perfectly still so its camouflage hides it. When it gets close enough to the prey, it charges forward. It then grabs the seal in its claws or teeth before the seal can escape back into the sea. Polar bears sometimes use this trick to catch young walrus, too.

Polar bears don't just attack animals on land. They can attack from the water as well. When they see an animal on the ice, they swim slowly toward the prey, using their front paws like paddles and their back paws to steer. At the edge of the ice, they quickly shoot up from the water to grab their unsuspecting prey.

Polar bears often hunt prey from the edge of sea ice. The bear is camouflaged against the ice, which makes it hard for prey to see.

A polar bear's blubber helps it to float so it can move along with its head above water, looking for prey.

Walrus also use their tusks to try to defend themselves against predators.

Links in the Food Chain

Walrus use their 3-foot-(1 m) long tusks to pull themselves onto the ice to rest. They dive to catch shellfish near the dark ocean floor. Walrus use their sensitive whiskers to feel for prey in the dark.

13

STILL HUNTING

Polar bears also catch prey by "still hunting." First, they use their excellent sense of smell to find a seal's **breathing hole**. This is a hole that a seal digs in the ice so it can come up for air while swimming. Then the polar bear crouches down near the hole and waits, patiently, silently, and without moving.

When a seal pushes its nose up through the hole, the waiting bear grabs it quickly with its giant paw and drags it out onto the ice. Sometimes the bear thrusts its head into the hole, catching prey in its sharp teeth. Polar bears can even catch 13-foot-(4 m) long beluga whales using this hunting trick!

A polar bear usually only has to wait for up to an hour for a seal to appear, but it will wait much longer if needed.

14

Links in the Food Chain

Belugas are white whales that feed on fish, shellfish, and worms. They look for prey on the ocean floor by shooting a jet of water from their mouths. This uncovers animals hiding in the sand or silt.

The beluga, or white whale, is one of the smallest types of whale.

Polar bears reach their long necks into smaller breathing holes to snatch prey.

ATTACKING DENS

It takes some time for polar bear cubs to build up the layer of blubber that protects them from the freezing Arctic Ocean. During this time, the mother bear hunts only on land, often looking for seals in dens. Female seals have their pups in dens they build under snow drifts.

A polar bear can smell seals in a den up to 3 feet (1 m) below even hard, thick snow. As soon as the bear senses prey in a den, it slowly stands up on its back legs. Then it crashes down with its front paws, using its heavy weight to smash through the roof of the den. It may take the bear several attempts to break into the den to catch prey inside.

In spring, female polar bears with young cubs often hunt by attacking seal dens.

KILLER FACT

Polar bear claws are thick, curved, very sharp, and over 2 inches (5 cm) long! The bear hooks its claws into heavy seals and their pups, then drags them out of their den or the ocean in an instant.

Polar bears use their powerful paws to smash into dens.

Hungry polar bear mothers and their cubs need the thick layer of fat on a seal pup's body.

FEASTING ON FAT

When a polar bear catches prey, it bites the animal on its head and neck to kill it. If the bear is near the water's edge, it drags its meal several feet (m) away to eat it. First, the bear eats the skin and blubber of the animal, then it eats the meat.

When there are plenty of prey animals around, polar bears only eat the blubber and skin of their prey. That's because skin and blubber have lots of **calories**. Calories give bears energy and help them to build up and keep their thick layer of blubber. A polar bear can eat 100 pounds (45 kg) of seal blubber at one meal!

While eating, polar bears often stop to wash themselves by rubbing their faces and fur in the snow.

KILLER FACT

Polar bears have 42 teeth. Their **canine** teeth are up to 2 inches (5 cm) long. The bear uses them to grip onto prey and tear tough skin. The bear's sharp **incisor** teeth rip off chunks of blubber and flesh. Polar bears use their back teeth to tear and chew meat.

The polar bear's sharp teeth are one of the features that make it a top predator.

SAVING ENERGY

After a polar bear eats a large animal it can rest for days. A ringed seal weighing 121 pounds (55 kg) can give a bear enough energy to rest for eight days before it needs to hunt again. Big animals use up a lot of energy whenever they move, so it is important that they rest when they can.

Even on days when they go hunting, most polar bears sleep for seven to eight hours at a time. They often take naps, too. On cold days, they sleep in pits in the snow with their backs toward the wind. Snow piles up on top of the bears, acting like a blanket to keep them warm.

On warmer days, polar bears sleep on top of the ground or ice.

On colder days, polar bears sleep in shallow pits they dig in the snow.

Links in the Food Chain

Polar bears also save energy by eating the **carcasses** of whales, seals, and walrus that they find. The bears can smell large carcasses from miles (km) away! By eating animals that are already dead, polar bears save energy that they would otherwise spend hunting live prey.

Polar bear mothers usually give birth to twin cubs in November or December. They have their babies in snow caves that they dig in snowdrifts. Here the cubs are safe from the harsh winter weather. Newborn polar bear cubs are about the size of a guinea pig. They are born blind, deaf, toothless, and totally helpless!

Cubs stay in the den with their mother for around three months. They quickly grow by **suckling** calorie-rich milk from their mother's body. By March or April the cubs are big and strong enough to leave the den and follow their mother as she hunts for food. Cubs stay with their mother for around two years.

Playing and wrestling together helps polar bear cubs build skills that will make them strong hunters.

KILLER FACT

Polar bears learn quickly because they are very smart and have a very large brain for their body size. These curious animals have good memories and are as intelligent as chimpanzees and gorillas.

Polar bear cubs follow and watch their mother when she hunts. By doing so, they learn the skills they need to become top of the food chain, too.

Polar bear cubs grow quickly on their mother's fat-rich milk and on seal blubber.

23

FOLLOWING PREY

Polar bears hunt from the edge of sea ice, using it as a platform from which to catch seals swimming in the ocean or resting on the sea ice. In summer, the edges of the sea ice melt. Then polar bears must travel north to follow the the ice and the prey that lives on it. In winter, when the sea ice increases again, the bears travel south to stay near the spreading edge of the ice.

Polar bears can swim long distances, and for days at a time. However, this uses a lot of energy. The bears can see well underwater, so they dive to catch food for energy when they can. They also catch seabirds sitting on the water by swimming up beneath them.

Polar bears climb onto platforms of ice floating on the water to rest when they can.

Links in the Food Chain

Ivory gulls are seabirds that live in the Arctic all year round. They walk along the ice edge and cracks in ice, looking for signs of Arctic cod and other fish. When the birds see a fish, they use their beaks to snatch it from the water.

Polar bears can swim 100 miles (160 km) without climbing out onto the ice to rest!

BEAR DANGERS

The biggest danger to polar bears is **climate change**. The Arctic is getting warmer and this is making the sea ice melt and break sooner than it usually does. Polar bears now have to swim longer distances to hunt, which means they go without food for long periods of time. Some starve on the ice. Others run out of energy and drown while swimming huge distances to try to find food.

As it becomes harder to find food, more polar bears may sniff out food farther inland. Some even enter villages and towns to find it. This brings the bears into contact with people, who may kill them out of fear, even though polar bear attacks on humans are very rare.

*Polar bears need the sea ice, but it is melting because of climate change. Polar bears are now one of the Earth's most endangered **mammals**.*

Links in the Food Chain

Polar bears do not fear humans, which makes them dangerous. A single swipe of a large male polar bear's paw could be enough to kill a person. Polar bears have been known to eat humans that they kill.

Polar bears are top of the food chain in the Arctic so the only other animals that kill them are humans.

NO MORE BEARS?

If there were no polar bears at the top of the food chain, it would affect all living things in the food chain. Without polar bears, the number of seals in the Arctic would very quickly grow. The seals would eat many more fish, which would affect other fish-eating predators, including people!

Polar bear leftovers are also an important supply of food for many Arctic animals. When polar bears eat only the skin and blubber of an animal, birds, Arctic foxes, and other animals eat the rest. Without polar bears, there would be no leftovers for these animals to eat. Without these easy meals, some would die.

Some people are working to protect the mighty polar bears and their vulnerable cubs to make sure they are around in the future.

Links in the Food Chain

The Arctic fox has gray fur in summer and thick, white fur in winter. It feeds on lemmings, voles, squirrels, birds, bird eggs, berries, fish, and dead animals. In winter, it often follows polar bears, hoping to eat their leftovers. During the winter, some Arctic foxes live on leftover meals from the polar bear.

Arctic foxes and many other animals rely on the existence of polar bears to help them survive, too.

GLOSSARY

algae (AL-jee) Simple, plantlike living things usually found in water.

Arctic (ARK-tik) An area made up of the ice-covered Arctic Ocean and surrounding land, including Greenland and the northern parts of Alaska, Canada, Norway, and Russia.

blubber (BLUH-ber) A layer of fat between the skin and muscle of most sea mammals.

breathing hole (BREE-thing HOHL) A hole that seals dig in the ice so they can come up for air when underwater.

calories (KA-luh-reez) The units of energy contained in food and drink.

camouflages (KA-muh-flahjez) When something is hard to see because its coloring blends into the surroundings.

canine (KAY-nyn) Long, pointed teeth in a predator's upper jaw.

carcasses (KAR-kus-ez) Dead animals.

climate change (KLY-mut CHAYNJ) The rise in temperature of the Earth's atmosphere, probably caused by human activities such as driving cars.

energy (EH-ner-jee) The power to live, grow, and move.

food chain (FOOD CHAYN) Living things connected because they are one another's food.

habitat (HA-buh-tat) The natural environment in which a living thing is found.

incisor (in-SY-zur) A narrow-edged tooth at the front of an animal's mouth.

insulation (in-suh-LAY-shun) Something that stops heat from escaping.

mammals (MA-muls) Animals that have fur or hair, give birth to live young, and feed their young on milk from the mother's body.

predators (PREH-duh-terz) Animals that hunt other animals for food.

prey (PRAY) Animals that are hunted by other animals for food.

stalking (STOK-ing) Chasing or approaching prey silently and secretly.

suckling (SUK-ling) Taking milk from a mother's body.

zooplankton (zoh-uh-PLANK-tun) Tiny animals that drift in the oceans.

Meinking, Mary. *Polar Bear vs. Seal.* Predator vs. Prey. Chicago, IL: Heinemann-Raintree, 2011.

Owen, Ruth. *Polar Bears.* Dr. Bob's Amazing World of Animals. New York: Windmill Books, 2012.

Rodríguez, Ana María. *Polar Bears, Penguins, and Other Mysterious Animals of the Extreme Cold.* Extreme Animals in Extreme Environments. Berkeley Heights, NJ: Enslow Publishers, 2012.

Wojahn, Rebecca Hogue, and Donald Wojahn. *A Tundra Food Chain: A Who-Eats-What Adventure in the Arctic.* Follow That Food Chain. Minneapolis, MN: Lerner Publications Company, 2009.

WEBSITES

For web resources related to the subject of this book, go to: www.windmillbooks.com/weblinks and select this book's title.

INDEX